)edication

his Self-Care Guide was created for those who feel guilty when they are not busy. Those who eel guilty when they take time for themselves by relaxing. Hopefully you find a balance in your fe that allows you to feel refreshed, empowered and fulfilled. Remember, it's Okay to relax, as will help you to become a better "you", before you can be a better "supporter" to someone else. igned, Latasha Strawder, LMFT

Special Thanks..

o my family, friends, colleagues for all of your support, kindness, and thoughtfulness. ou are apart of my "self-care" and I'm very thankful for you.

Publisher: TRY Speaking Up Media & Publishing, LLC.

ISBN: 9798988522607
Please be advised that this self-care guide is for educational purposes only,
and is not all inclusive to all of the forms of self-care that can
be helpful to each person. Please note this book should be used as a guide, and not
all inclusive to all things mental health, self-care and health.
This guide is not to be used in place of professional services (i.e., therapy, seeing a health professional, etc.).
s guide should be used along with other methods of self-care for educational purposes and entertainment solely.

Made in the USA

WWW.TRYTUTORINGSERVICES.COM

Order book
in Print

@TRY.TUTORING.COPING.SOLUTIONS

Self Care

THE PRACTICE OF TAKING ACTION TO PRESERVE OR IMPROVE ONE'S OWN HEALTH

RELAX TODAY, OKAY?

I WILL GET TO IT TOMORROW

MY MENTAL HEALTH MATTERS TOO

I WILL BE PATIENT WITH MYSELF

I NEED TO BE MORE KIND TO MYSELF

IT'S OKAY TO STOP AND REFLECT

I GIVE MYSELF PERMISSION TO RELAX TODAY

OVERWORKING MYSELF WILL NOT HELP LONGTERM

I GIVE MYSELF PERMISSION TO IMPROVE MY WELL-BEING

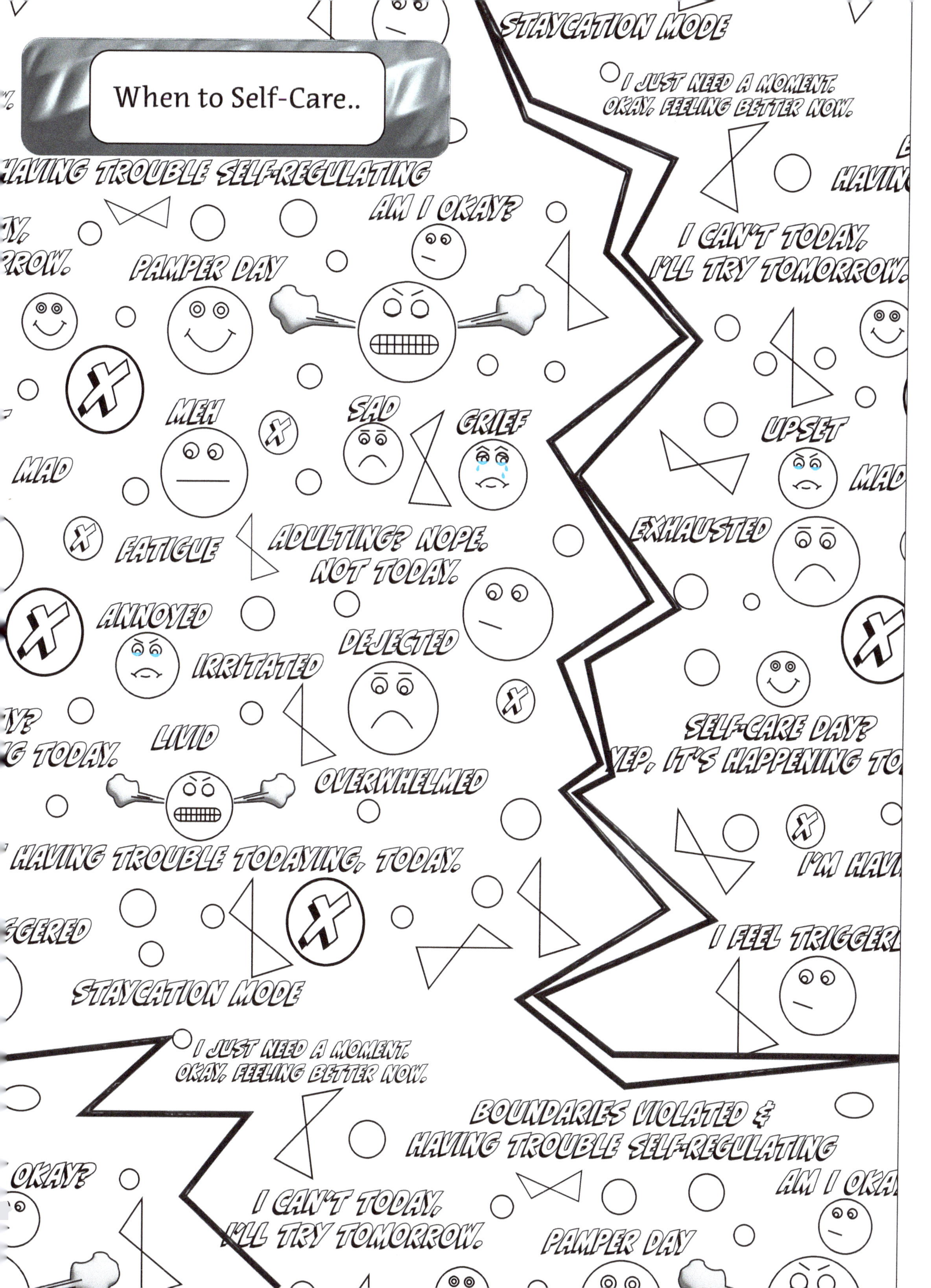
When to Self-Care..
STAYCATION MODE
I JUST NEED A MOMENT. OKAY, FEELING BETTER NOW.
AM I OKAY?
PAMPER DAY
I CAN'T TODAY, I'LL TRY TOMORROW.
MEH
SAD
GRIEF
UPSET
MAD
EXHAUSTED
FATIGUE
ADULTING? NOPE. NOT TODAY.
ANNOYED
IRRITATED
DEJECTED
SELF-CARE DAY?
LIVID
OVERWHELMED
HAVING TROUBLE TODAYING, TODAY.
STAYCATION MODE
I JUST NEED A MOMENT. OKAY, FEELING BETTER NOW.
BOUNDARIES VIOLATED & HAVING TROUBLE SELF-REGULATING
I CAN'T TODAY, I'LL TRY TOMORROW.
PAMPER DAY

MY STABILITY SCALE

Self-Care means checking in with myself

0 1 2 3 4 5 6 7 8 9 10

icidal day

Neutral

Extremely Happy in MY Life Today

OBSERVATIONS ABOUT MYSELF WHEN I'M MENTALLY STABLE

OBSERVATIONS ABOUT MYSELF WHEN I'M NOT MENTALLY STABLE

*Suicide Prevention Hotline, text crisis to "988" or dial "988". My life matters 

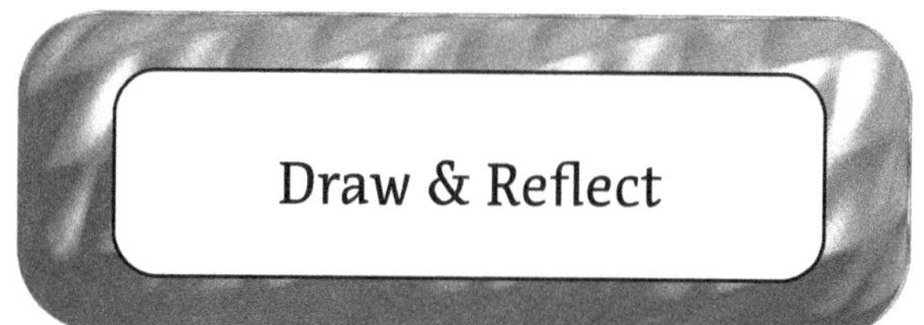

THINGS I NEED IN MY LIFE TO HAVE MENTAL STABILITY..

WAYS I CAN MAKE THIS SUSTAINABLE, LONG-TERM?

Mental Instability for me looks like...

THINGS I NEED TO REMOVE FROM MY LIFE TO HAVE LESS MENTAL INSTABILITY..

WAYS I CAN MAKE THIS SUSTAINABLE, LONG-TERM?

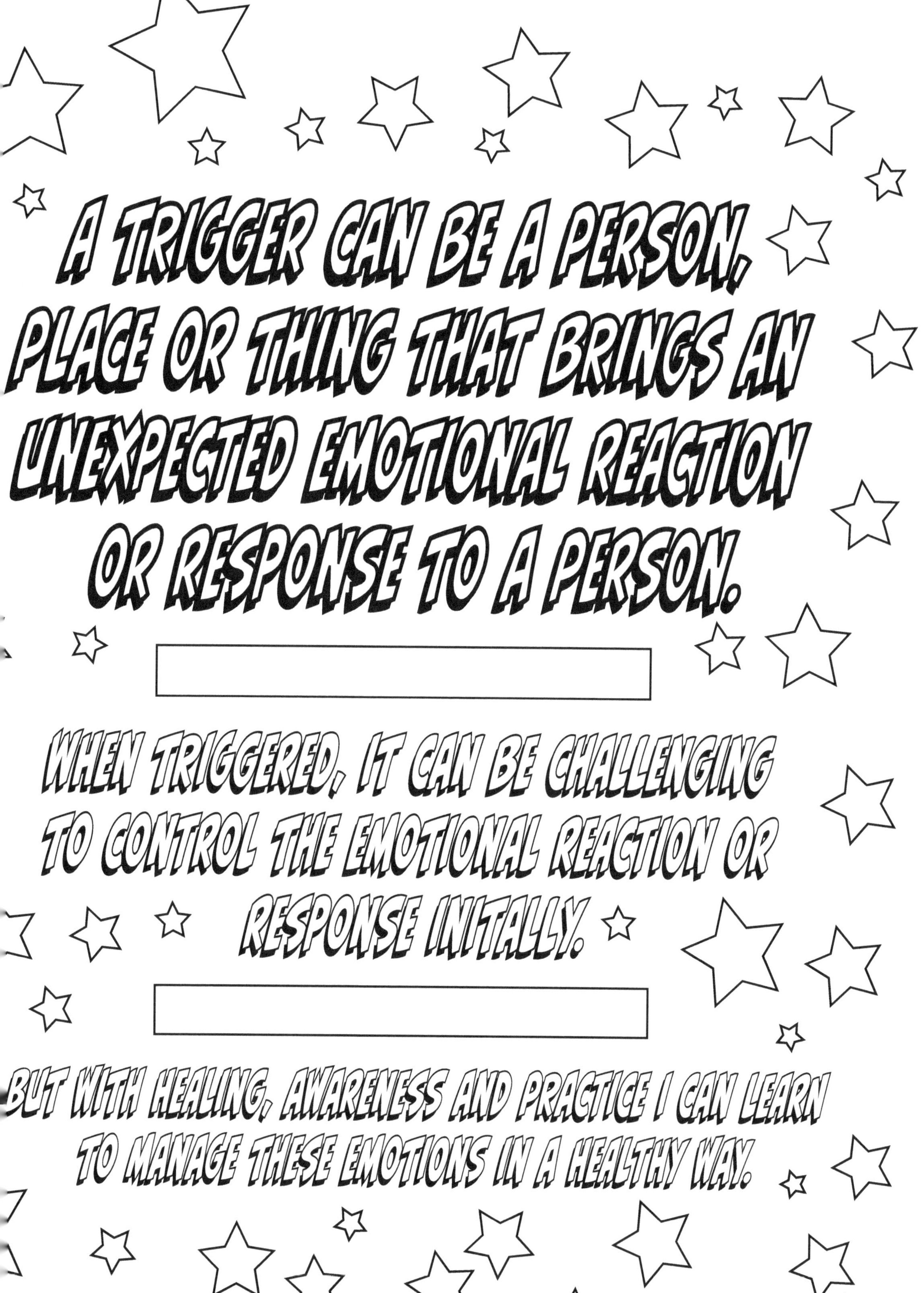
A TRIGGER CAN BE A PERSON, PLACE OR THING THAT BRINGS AN UNEXPECTED EMOTIONAL REACTION OR RESPONSE TO A PERSON.
WHEN TRIGGERED, IT CAN BE CHALLENGING TO CONTROL THE EMOTIONAL REACTION OR RESPONSE INITALLY.
BUT WITH HEALING, AWARENESS AND PRACTICE I CAN LEARN TO MANAGE THESE EMOTIONS IN A HEALTHY WAY.

TYPES OF TRIGGERS

OLFACTORY

PERFUME

ALCOHOL

FOOD

DESSERTS

DRUGS

COLOGNE

SCENTS

VISUAL

WATCHING T.V.

MOVIES

AUTOMOBILES

REACTIONS

RIENDS

HOMES

FAMILIES

RESTARAUNTS

APPEARANCE

BODY LANGUAGE

FACIAL EXPRESSIONS

URNITURE

CLOTHING

PEOPLE

LOCATIONS

SYMBOLS

NIMALS

PLACES

TYPES OF FOOD

SHOES

PHYSICAL

EATING

HUNGER

MOOD

TOUCH

VIOLENCE

FEELINGS

TEMPERATURES

INTIMACY

ABUSE

DRUGS

TEXTURES

BODY SENSATIONS

FOOD

PAIN

TASTE

DRINKING

AUDITORY

NTRUSIVE THOUGHTS

SONGS

MEMORIES

PHRASES

SILENCE

OVIES

YELLING/SCREAMING

ORDS

MUSIC

FACIALS
WASH DAY!
MANI
MASSAGE
RELAX
PEDI
REPEAT
REPEAT
REST DAY
ASH DAY!
PAMPER
SELF-CARE
TAKE IT EASY
REPEAT
LIVE
ANOTHER
DAY

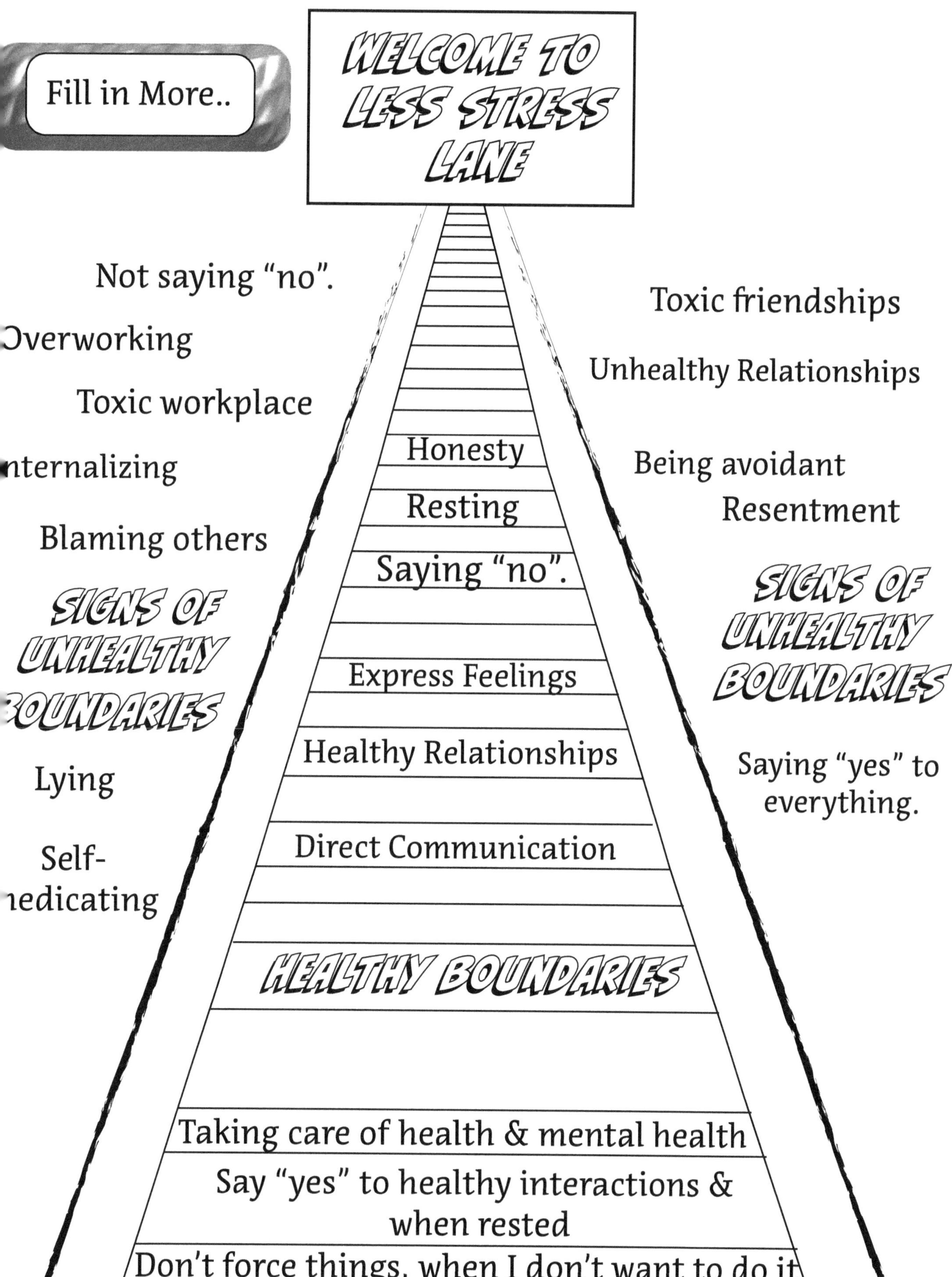

Fill in More..
WELCOME TO LESS STRESS LANE
Not saying "no".
Overworking
Toxic workplace
Internalizing
Blaming others
SIGNS OF UNHEALTHY BOUNDARIES
Lying
Self-medicating
Toxic friendships
Unhealthy Relationships
Being avoidant
Resentment
SIGNS OF UNHEALTHY BOUNDARIES
Saying "yes" to everything.
Honesty
Resting
Saying "no".
Express Feelings
Healthy Relationships
Direct Communication
HEALTHY BOUNDARIES
Taking care of health & mental health
Say "yes" to healthy interactions & when rested
Don't force things, when I don't want to do it.

EXERCISE

SELF-CARE

SMILE

FUN IN THE SUN

HERAPY

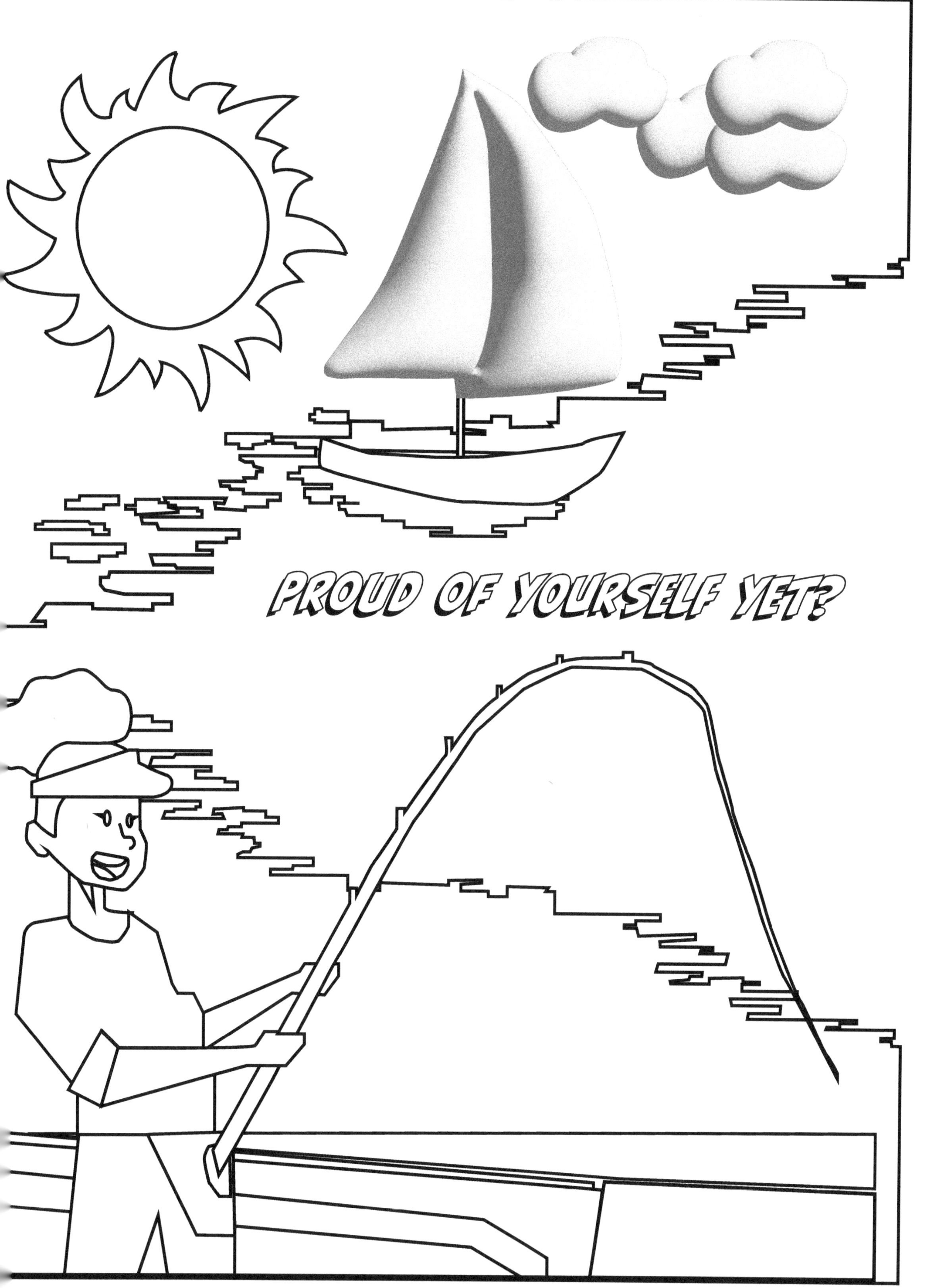
PROUD OF YOURSELF YET?

FISHERMANS WHARF
OF SAN FRANCISCO
YEP, I'M PROUD OF MYSELF

OMG! Self care is the best care!
HOME!

MENTAL HEALTH
GROW
HEAL
STAY CALM
GROW
STAY CALM
RELAX
CHILL
RELAX
STAY CALM
MENTAL HEALTH
CHILL
HOME!
OMG!
Self care
is the
best care!
YOUR TURN!

SOLITUDE
Z's
Z's
HAHA
TALK WITH A SUPPORT PERSON
TALK WITH A SUPPORT PERSON
THERAPY
THERAPY
MENTAL HEALTH
RELAX
RELAX
SELF-CARE
VACATION
SOLITUDE
SOLITUDE
Z's
HAHA
HAHA
TALK WITH A SUPPORT PERSON
THERAPY
RELAX
VACATION
VACATION
SOLITUDE

HAHA
TALK WITH A SUPPORT PERSON
HIKE
RUN
HEALTHY EATING
RELAX
WALK
SPA
VACATION
SOLITUDE
SWIM
MANI
PEDI
MASSAGE

MAKE TRY RESTORATION COPING
SKILL BRACELETS!
Lavender
BREATHE

www.ingramcontent.com/pod-product-compliance
Lightning Source LLC
LaVergne TN
LVHW081425110826
845149LV00010B/1873

* 9 7 9 8 9 8 8 5 2 2 6 0 7 *